One

Stephanie Johnston

BookLeaf
Publishing

India | USA | UK

Presentation by *BookLeaf Publishing*

Web: www.bookleafpub.com

E-mail: info@bookleafpub.com

ISBN: 978-93-5744-970-0

First edition 2022

DEDICATION

This book of poems is dedicated to all of my family and friends who allow me to be creative. Thank you for always helping me expand my knowledge and inspiring me! I would especially like to thank my parents who always believe in me and support my dreams. I would also like to dedicate this book to God, who guides me and has placed these words in my heart.

PREFACE

I hope you enjoy this book of poetry filled with ideas that stem from biblical teachings, life experiences, and the world around me. There is so much freedom in letting words dance on the page and I hope you can find some meaning in these words as well.

Silence

Silence
In a world of thunder
Hard to come by
But filled with wonder
The only sound heard
Is that of my mind
Words cut through
Like 10000 knifes
Breath is stolen
And brain on fire
But nothing ever seems to tire
But when the silence truly comes
My soul refreshed
No longer numb

Believe

At first I believed
But then I forgot
I couldn't see
Other than what was taught
I believed the lies
That told me otherwise
But then I saw
In a might wave
You called me yours
And I believed that day
I was no longer afraid
Just redeemed in you
I once forgot
But now I see truth

Peace

One breath
One word
One song
Fills us up with peace
One day
One thought
One love
Like one big hug
Each little thing
That you give to us
Fills us up with peace
And results in love

Grace

Here we stand
Two ways to go
Back to shame
Or forward in Hope
The war inside
It rages on
But your grace is always strong
So on the day
The battle was fought
You took my heart
And pulled me up
You give your grace
And give your love
I am found in you
Your grace is always strong

Joy

One day I sat
I heard you call
The joy I felt
Because shame was gone
I knew you cared
You had called me home
You filled me up
I was not alone
Joy came over
Like a rushing wave
I finally believed
I was finally saved

Prayer

In the quiet of the morning
Or the chaos of the day
I call out your name
And find peace regained
My anxious heart
Gripped in your love
I take a deep breath
And feel your precious touch
The prayer I pray
Goes out to you
It holds inside
My greatest truths
Truth of pain
Truth of love
And one more truth
Of the one above
I pray to you God
The one above
That all these things
Will forever be

Strength

Strength in patience
Strength in trust
Strength in the one who never gives up
His mercy is great
All shame at his feet
Even in the shadows
His message is complete
I am not be perfect
But I find strength in him
He gives me the power
To look towards him

Hope

Broken people
That need to be healed
A broken world
That needs a great shield
The world needs hope
Hope found in you
Hope for the day
That we look to you
Hope when we're hurting
Hope when we're free
Hope in affliction
In hope that we see
Look towards you
In all that we do
Hope in your love
Your grace, that stands true

Healing

A heart shattered in shame
No belief of love ever the same
Feeling like I failed
Always holding like in jail
I never knew your love
Until your hands reached my heart
You sent your army
You sent your flood
You healed me up
And showed me love

Shame

Like an endless cycle
Mind stuck on loop
Hiding from the love
That once held so true
Feeling so unworthy
Hiding in the shame
No one seems to see it
But it is felt in every way
Feeling like no end
Feeling like no truth
One day the words rush over
Shame can not hold you
Once you were afraid
Shame held you close
Felt like a comfort
But now you must let go
The pain tries to bind you
And whisper comforting words
But take a stand away
And let go of shames hand

Forward

One step in the right direction
One step towards the goal
One step towards the truth
One step to keep the gold
There is no time to weary
There is no time to wait
But there is time
To go forward in faith

Redeemed

Lost in a past of fear
Felt like no one could hear
But then you called us out
And saved us from our doubt
Patiently waiting for your child
To find their way to you
For when we call your name
You redeem us with your grace

Fear

Alone
In thought
My mind races
I try to hide
I have no clear direction
All I have is fear inside
It holds like flame to a candle
And makes doubt my closest friend
I try to get away
From fear that stays
I stand plagued
Scared, afraid
Alone

View

I always wanted to be
Like the girls in the movies
Perfect hair
Perfect smile
Sure of who they were
Looking at myself
Through too much broken glass
I can't see
What you see
When you look at me

Perspective

In the mirror
There stands a girl
Tears in her eyes
Because she can't let go
Let go of what the world has said
Or find good words inside her head
She works to change the way she sees
A new perspective she works to read
She looks in the mirror
And now she sees
A changed perspective
And a new belief

Freedom

Freedom is like running
Running with no fear
Running through the forest
Where all you hear is clear
Freedom in the anguish
When all the hope seems lost
But freedom comes
Like trumpet sound
And nothing could ever stop

Run

Run the race before you
With eyes fixed ahead
There is nothing that can stop you
On this journey up ahead
Yes it may seem scary
Yes it will be tough
But just keep on running
Until you find your stride above

Love

Love burns like a fire
It is warm, and keeps you safe
But other times
It takes a toll
And ruins a great scape
Love can be forgotten
But love is always near
When a path is broken
The fire still finds a clear
The fire of love rages through
And makes new paths
Makes our hearts new

Broken

Tiny hands
Gentle heart
Filled with strength
Not yet grown up
But then the world
Shows what it hides
The little girl is left to cry
But then she finds out who she is
Once was broken, but now shows no fear

Fight

No one answer
No one way
We have to fight
To see our day
The paths are scary
The loads aren't light
We bear the burden
Through the night
Fight from the shadows
That hide your will
Fight from the depths
Where you stayed still
No longer scared
Of what the fight might bring
Go forward and fight
For the goal that sings

Truth

One last time
To hear the truth
You are loved
There is so much proof
You may not feel it
You may not see
But here I tell you
You can be
Be the one who fights the war
Be the one who always goes for
Goes for what they can not see
Goes for what they are told not to be
You fight the fight that rages on
And don't grow weary in what goes wrong
The path you take is wound for you
Wound by one who knows your truth